GW01607468

BLACK

HEART OF THE LIMERICK

Writing a limerick and 150 original limericks

Written and illustrated by

Christopher Woodger

From Christopher Woodger for Rachel.

ODYSSEY poets

ODYSSEY poets
Coleridge Cottage
Nether Stowey
Somerset

Printed in England

ISBN 1 897654 88 X

Dedicated to my beloved daughter Angela who has egged me on disgracefully.

"Written for you Edward Lear – you will die forever!"

A totally tummy-taut toad
quite quite fat enough to explode
sucked himself in
thinner than thin
and fell through a crack in the road

Ballooning in tune with the sky
what on earth does the moon signify?
mere air with a crust
just spherical dust
that spins to the fart of a fly ...

A man spoke these nightmarish notions
"My teardrops shrank larger than oceans ...
I found I had drowned
but blushed as the sound
was the gush of my rushing emotions"

Part

WRITING A LIMERICK

While verse could do worse as the priming
can man mate to its raciest rhyming?
... enticingly pissed
a poet twice missed
when his plot went to pot with the timing ...

INTRODUCTION

Writing verse can become as natural as breathing, an expression of the everlasting conversation we have with ourselves. Like a kind of thought diary. Children playing together sing out verses so vibrantly and spontaneously simply as an outlet for their bursting vitality.

Limericks too thump out their message in a rhythmic drumbeat of verse.

Starting from scratch my impulse was to write original limericks, not on the *filth for filth's sake* basis which has given this vivid, versatile verse form a bad name, but more on the *creative filth* (!) principle. Could limericks as they presently appear, extend into other forms – six liners?.. seven liners? and also be drawn from a whole range of new sources?

After years of chasing words through the night the first part of my book emerged – WRITING A LIMERICK, which shows, bit by bit, how anyone can give their own flavour to their own limericks .... a lasting delight! Part one concludes with thoughts on the illusive nature of the limerick and its uncertain history.

The second part, THE LIMERICKS, contains 150 out of a total of 450 written so far, and these are illustrated with about 30 of my own pen and ink drawings.

MY BACKGROUND AND HOW THE SEEDS WERE SOWN

Limericks are fiendishly difficult to write at first, but I was fortunate in my family background which encouraged a love of the English language. This served as an excellent basis for writing limericks.

My father loved playing about with words :

> The infernal Colonel, impartial Marshall and defective detective sat at an unstable table in a potential torrential
>
> All good unclean fun

And he introduced me to spoonerisms :

oiled bicycles – boiled icicles

beery wenches – weary benches

show me into a seat – sew me into a sheet

These have occurred to me :

madly bashed – badly mashed

mailed junk – jailed monk

male state – stalemate

unholed tights – untold heights

cats in a rage – rats in a cage

missing on the peak – pissing on the meek

the packed lunch lacked punch

four lettered words – law fettered words

Try these: boars head handy rug cunning stunt

WRITING PARODIES OF EXISTING VERSES

Long before I attempted my first limerick, I amused my daughters by writing parodies of verses written for children, an easier task than having to cope with inventing the content of the verse at the same time. This, taken from Lear's *The Owl and The Pussycat* :

"Dear pig are you willing
To sell for one shilling
Your ring?", Said the piggy, "I will".
So they took it away
And were married next day
By the turkey who lives on the hill.

became :

"Dear pig are you willing
To sell for one shilling
Your ring?", Said the piggy, "No fear!"
So they left it behind
With that pig so unkind
But attached to the side of his ear.

I have written more of these parodies to encourage you to write your own, both to amuse yourself and any children around and also as a preparation for embarking on the struggle to write your first limerick :

I love little pussy
Her coat is so warm
And if I don't hurt her
She'll do me no harm.
Her claws in my thigh
While my stockings do rend
If I keep quite quite still
Will come out in the end.

Mary had a little lamb, it followed her to school.
She nearly did detention – it broke a sacred rule.
Not deterred, that little lamb climbed upon a stool
And chalked advanced equations to show she was no fool.
The teacher stared astonished and turned a shade of red,
"Do as well in English – you'll be Assistant Head!"
Now a clever little lamb, perhaps a trifle wary,
Punctual at the old school gates, is followed by poor Mary.

TRYING OUT VERSE FORMS

This is a simple verse made up from scratch :

Those with wills of iron
and the ego of a lion
have iron hearts
and iron farts
... an iron bed to cry on

Here is a more complicated example, where lines one, two, five and six rhyme with *Minotaur,* and sandwiched in between are just two lines rhyming with *heel :*

To master the maze to the Minotaur
once took thirty-five days .. or more
arriving tired .. mired .. down at heel
barely enough for his evening meal.
Life's now become such a bum of a bore
we whip round express on a *Minotour*

THERE WAS AN OLD MAN WITH A BEARD

The great Edward Lear wrote :

> There was an Old Man with a beard,
> Who said, "It is just as I feared! –
> Two Owls and a Hen, four Larks and a Wren,
> Have all built their nests in my beard!"

It puzzled me from the moment I first heard this thrilling verse as a boy as to why? why? why? to the serious detriment of this limerick, he repeated *beard* – at the very point of climax!

Changing the rhythm and meaning slightly, with the emphasis coming on *man* and *just* and *feared,* he might have written :

> An Old Man said, "It's just as I feared! –
> With the world for their young to be reared,
> Two Owls and a Hen, four Larks and a Wren,
> Have all built their nests in my beard!"

Was *beard* repeated in the original version because no usable words could be found to rhyme with it?

Checking this out, I was amazed at the rich choice of words available to Lear, including :

tiered	geared	reared	weird
neared	cheered	eared	sneered
jeered	peered	veered	steered

Some Elizabethan verses only rhyme when spoken with a particular north country accent. As accents vary, it can be quite difficult to decide what does and doesn't rhyme. It shouldn't, however, be too difficult to improve on the rhyming in *Baa baa black sheep have you any wool?...* where *dame* and *lane* are paired ..... *m* and *n* definitely do not rhyme!

Every limerick has the potential for many variations. I have written ten to explore Lear's theme. This one follows on from the way he depicted himself as the old man with his arms thrust backwards and upwards, wing-like, and pointing towards the sky :

> How he flapped! ... and how rudely they jeered,
> "Some Old Men fly like Eagles!" they sneered,
> Two Owls and a Hen, four Larks and a Wren,
> With jests built their nests in his beard.

I prefer the rolling momentum of Lear's original version, but the value in having three rhyming lines compared to only two is decisive isn't it? Yet Lear stuck to his method tenaciously. Frequently the whole of the first line reappears tamely again, only slightly changed, as the last line.

An alternative last line would be :

Were guests in their nests in his beard.

Another two versions :

An Old Man cried, "Not one shall be spared!
They think I'm just here to be shared –
Two Owls and a Hen, four Larks and a Wren,
will nest in their best in my beard!"

An Old Man cried, "The din they have dared!
Not once have my poor nerves been spared!
Two Owls and a Hen, four Larks and a Wren,
Put their best to the test in my beard."

Here is a rare example of Lear using three long rhyming lines :

> There was an Old Man who supposed,
> That the street door was partially closed;
> But some very large rats, ate his coats and his hats,
> While that futile Old Gentleman dozed.

Does the second *old* add anything to this verse? Isn't it being used as a filler-word whose sole function is to ensure the right number of syllables in the line? An important point when everything has to be compressed into just five lines ... each word like a little gold nugget.

Lear's book of nonsense verses written for children popularised limericks, though he did not invent them. He often used only one syllable words, as in *The Old Man with a beard.*

Lear started writing Limericks when a friend suggested as a first line:

> There was an Old Man from Tobago

Using an alternative location, such as

> There was an Old Man from Dundee

would have provided a greater choice of useful rhyming words:

be me he we three tea flea twee agree glee knee etc.

One must always go by the sound of the rhyming words and try not to be put off by the amazing variety and the truly creative spelling to be found in the English language. All these words rhyme :

awe boar bore caw door drawer or tour war whore hoar

Sometimes only three rhyming words are available to you but there is real creative potential in having words, as it were, thrust upon you, forcing you into a mental dexterity you had no idea you possessed.

INSPIRATION FOR A LIMERICK

Limericks can spring from an idea or an event experienced personally, invented perhaps, or read in a book or newspaper. They can equally well start from a bouncing string of words, rhythmically satisfying, with an ending you will be able to find other appropriate words to rhyme with.

It was announced on the radio that a girl, floating on a rubber airbed shaped like a swan, had been swept out to sea. She was saved by a young man who bravely rode to rescue her on an inflatable crayfish.

Such a superb example of natural surrealism is irresistible to a writer of limericks, so I set out on the first task – discovering just which rhyming words might tell this story :

Discouragingly, *swan* didn't seem to rhyme with very much :

on wan gone upon don con

Nor did *crayfish* prove to be very promising, either :

dish wish swish

With this story always in mind the range needed to be extended. I came up with :

giraffe which at least gave me *laugh*

bee rhymed with *sea* and *free* along with much else.

The first two long rhyming lines could now be written :

Once an overblown girl swept to sea
on an airbed shaped just like a bee

The two short middle lines could then be added :

... she was let down – don't laugh!
by a leaking giraffe

The two short lines must match each other in their rhythm, rhyme and scansion. If the long lines grow, so too can the short lines, while keeping their relative lengths.

Adding the final long line to complement the first two paired long lines, the limerick is complete :

Once an overblown girl swept to sea
on an airbed shaped just like a bee
... she was let down – don't laugh!
by a leaking giraffe
though the rubberised coastguard was free!

The terms `long line´ and `short line´ refer to the number of syllables in the line, as these determine its rhythm, rather than the number of words or letters per line, which are irrelevant.

COUNTING THE SYLLABLES

As limerick writing develops, one senses whether one has a syllable too few or too many in a line. Paired verses can vary slightly in the number of syllables per line. But it can help a lot to count all the syllables and underline the stressed ones :

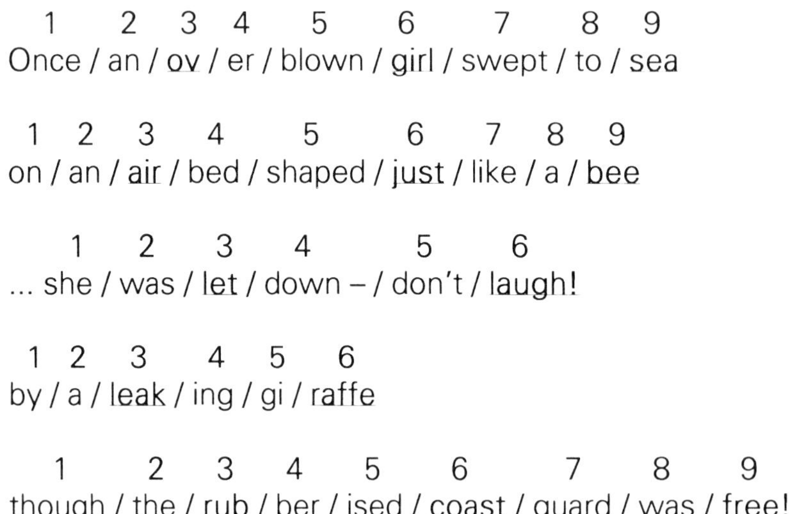

1 2 3 4 5 6 7 8 9
Once / an / ov / er / blown / girl / swept / to / sea

1 2 3 4 5 6 7 8 9
on / an / air / bed / shaped / just / like / a / bee

1 2 3 4 5 6
... she / was / let / down – / don't / laugh!

1 2 3 4 5 6
by / a / leak / ing / gi / raffe

1 2 3 4 5 6 7 8 9
though / the / rub / ber / ised / coast / guard / was / free!

The underlined syllables show the typical stress pattern of a limerick : three in the long lines and two in the short lines. The position of the stressed syllables can be varied to some extent – note that in *There was an Old Man with a beard* the first stressed syllable is the second one.

Here is an amusing lesson in scansion, not my own, rewritten from memory with modifications :

A poet whose work ran and ran
sighed, "My verses seem never to scan
my pen starts to race
and I run out of space
soIcramasmanywordsintothelastlineasIpossiblycan".

The original version used *Japan* solely to rhyme with `scan´ despite its utter irrelevance!

It is the hardest thing imaginable to match the idea contained in a brilliant limerick and the way this idea is expressed, with perfect rhyming, scansion and appropriate stress. It is all too easy for the stress in a word to fall on a different syllable from the naturally occurring stress when it is spoken. But every verse can be unique with its own form, tempo and rhythmic character.

If I had stuck to only one rhythmic form with the idea that all limericks had to follow the same pattern, this book would have become repetitive and dreary.

Especially with ambitious limericks, one needs one or two preliminary readings to get a feeling for the emphasis required for key syllables.

THOUGHTS ON WRITING A LIMERICK

As you write your first limerick, climbing Everest will seem to be the easier option, but when you have written one verse, six can follow and when you have written six, you can write sixty or four hundred. Starting to write from cold is very difficult, as it is only by reading and writing limericks that your brain cells fall into the appropriate way of rhythmical thinking.

Limerick writing in any quantity improves your mental agility and your memory to an unbelievable degree. It becomes quite possible to compose these verses entirely in your mind.

You don't need a degree in English either. I was bottom in almost all known subjects at school ... a love of limericks is enough, plus determination bordering on a kind of divine madness. That's all!

It's worth always carrying pen and paper for recording ideas which somehow seem to occur at the most inconvenient moments. I only used a word-processor to finalise the font, to work out the spacing and to do something about the horrendous spelling mistakes. What effect, I wonder, might computers have in the future, on the writing of limericks?

"If only to prove I'm no dick
I'll compute my own limerick"
he titters, "Bloody rumour
I've got no sodding humour!"
... the print-out reads – PRICK! PRICK! PRICK! PRICK!

(The number of syllables per line here is : 8 ... 8 ... 7 ... 7 ... 8)

When you write your first good one, it will make up for many many groanings, gnashings and failures :

A writer with no-one to blame
yelled, "My poems are SO bloody tame!
when I'm seized by a spasm
a creative orgasm
they still look the same fucking same"

(Syllables per line : 8 ... 9 ... 7 ... 7 ... 8)

At first I tried *bloody* in the last line when I was writing this limerick but the emphasis needed to be stronger. *Fucking* it simply had to be, having fuck-all to do with decency and everything to do with getting the fucking thing right!

A limerick grows as continuous changes are made to the first roughed out version, which might even have holes in it, waiting for a possible word with the right number of syllables to be added later. The number of changes a verse goes through to attain real quality though is astonishing, but I have suffered not a moment of boredom in writing them – JUST AGONY!

Examples of the kind of changes and developments that do occur :

A torrent of pure pig's ear claptrap
trapped a dog attempting a catnap
but with bitching so catty
half cuckoo half batty
he chased the bitch out through the cat-flap

Pig's ear was simply stuck in there hastily to keep the rhythm going until something better could be found. Time can pass before a new development occurs to you. As verses can pass lightly through your thoughts, without you being fully aware that this is even happening, many limericks can be worked on over the same period. This version finally saw the light :

A bitch's dire dogged damn claptrap
trapped a dog in the bog for a catnap
.. sunk from bewitching
to blood-boiling bitching
he hitched .. pitched her .. ditched – through the cat-flap

While the first line words thump across the page, those in the last line are slowed right down. Sometimes if one wishes, one can keep the verse flowing on with no break from start to finish so that the whole story can be told in a single sentence :

> DELIGHTED with being so dead!
> a suicide flew from his bed
> in the shape of his soul
> as it rushed from its role
> through the hole in his unholy head

I was quite pleased with :

> Halfway through a vexed sexual party
> those girls from the top clitorati
> were hot to determine
> with barely a sperm in
> who's the most arty ... stroke ... tarty

Then this turned up :

> A rumpty! tumptly! humpty! pumpty! party
> twenty tip-top girls a tad too arty
> hot! hot! to determine
> with barely a sperm in
> who? who? who? .. the true clued .. clitorati?

The presumably entirely new word *clitorati* was born when I misheard *glitterati* spoken on a radio programme! ... and wrote it down.

You will find additional rhyming words – internal rhyming – can sometimes be found to enrich your verse and these help keep up the forward pressure. So far this is my best example :

We could and we should be aghast
this car age – outrageously fast!
from the need for such speed
we indeed must be freed
... but not one finds it fun to be last

Alliteration – the repetition of words starting with the same letter has a similar value: for example *lovely little lissom Lazuli.* (A line from one of my limericks).

Punctuation requires vital personal decisions. As each line of verse is separate and provides a tiny natural break, full stops can be avoided if you wish. Two or three dots used at either end of a line, rather than the abrupt interruption of a full stop, ensures continuity. When speed is important no punctuation at all is a possibility. On the other hand you might need a real battery of visually exciting punctuation marks firing off! It's a question of using what is most appropriate.

Here is an example of a limerick where a second version suggested itself :

Garden gnomes as they fish plastic pools
look embarrassed to death .. the poor fools!
they wait and they wait
in a neurotic state
welded by cramp to their stools

Garden gnomes as they fish plastic pools
look embarrassing blithering fools!
their brains might work faster
if they weren't made of plaster —
rods break and they all use their tools

I have found on occasion a limerick has appeared fully fledged between putting the coffee on and finishing the first cup, and so at times there are no rewrites at all. Thirty is pretty normal however.

Limericks thrive on pushing themselves to the limit but there has to be some ultimate justification, some inner truth or a particularly funny idea, to back them up.

Without an underlying meaning, even superbly flowing words or immaculate rhyming and scanning will come to nothing. You need to be very clear what the essential message of your limerick is, focusing all the words accordingly. This basic meaning may or may not be crystal clear when you start writing a verse. It sometimes evolves gradually as the verse itself evolves. Both alternatives are equally valid.

The message in the following example warns the reader not to accept myths uncritically – the devil, if he exists, might be multi-coloured. In this instance the idea was formed in my head before I started writing the limerick :

A soul just returned from the dead
said, "The Devil is violet and red
purplish too
green.. yellow.. blue
with a rainbow instead of a head"

A common fault in limerick writing occurs when a stressed syllable is in the wrong position within the line :

As the light was beginning to fade
a boy thrashed to the distant girl's aid
she snapped at him glaring
"Mermaids hate boys staring
not tonight – my nerves are too frayed!"

The stress when *Mermaid* is spoken falls on the first syllable, *Mer,* but in this limerick the stress should be on *maid,* which makes it sound rather artificial – and most uncomfortable. The problem in this case could be solved with :

"We mermaids hate staring

An alternative last line might be :

PISS OFF! ... I don't want to be laid!"

At one point while writing a limerick, a third short line just mysteriously appeared by accident :

"That hand with a sword in the lake"
moaned Arthur, "An epic mistake!
I shouldn't ask why
as indeed so am I –
just pie in the sky
a transparent legendary fake"

From then on I watched out for the opportunity of using this extra line. Finding the extra rhyming word made things harder of course. Even when an appropriate word was waiting to be used, the limerick in question sometimes needed the economy you get with just five lines.

You also have to be careful with these longer verses that the meaning contained in the final line doesn't become isolated from the content of the first two lines. I was nevertheless delighted with the discovery. Whether these six-liners should be called limericks though, I leave it to you to decide. I believe they should be, myself.

The art of limerick writing lies in marrying the technical side – where you sit at a table slogging through the dictionary and rhyming dictionary, trying out dozens of ways of expressing an idea – with the intuitive side of our nature. This is the partly unconscious, creative side of ourselves which beavers away quietly until sometimes a whole line flashes unbidden into our consciousness ... as though it was written by someone else.

Here's another possibility – the limerick as serious poetry :

I passed close to a fox in the night
as he silently shadowed from sight
a once-for-all meeting
so precious so fleeting
at the edge of perpetual light

And a very different version :

I passed close by a fox in the night
as he shadowed from alien sight
a car-light-caught meeting –
the glance without greeting
a chilling and soulless delight!

I gave a limerick reading to two friends, asking them to list thirty verses in order of preference, as a test of how well they might be received. The limerick at the top of the first friend's list appeared at the bottom of the other's. This was the verse in question :

Stonehenge before they burned candles
before we even wore sandals
had lasted for ages
revered by the sages
... now the loo's smashed up by the vandals

So if one person doesn't react positively to your work, don't despair....

Don't get depressed with all your rejected attempts, either, as they are an essential part of the creative process. To write six limericks at all is a real achievement and they are bound to improve immeasurably in time.

It is quite extraordinarily difficult to judge success and failure in one's own work. Certainly, you can't be creative and critical of your writing at the same time.

The best approach to writing your own limericks, as in all forms of creativity, is to set out to reinvent them fearlessly without being crippled by the dire negative influences embedded in our culture.

PUSHING BACK THE BOUNDARIES

For myself I was curious to know :

Could I eliminate the names of people and places
and so free space for the unfolding drama?

Can a limerick express an opinion as distinct from telling a story?

Could I extend the range of sources from which limericks have traditionally been drawn?

Can limericks be mysterious ... or relatively serious?

Can the structure of a limerick be changed, developed?

Could I, like Edward Lear, both write and illustrate a book containing only fresh material – a refreshing change these days from endlessly recycled compilations?

The answer in every case was YES! YES! YES! – but how successfully you can decide for yourself.

THE ILLUSIVE NATURE OF LIMERICKS

At the heart of the limerick lies the closely linked relationship between narrative, rhythm, rhyme and humour. The parts of the story to be told must be set out in their logical order with each word carrying exactly the right meaning. The limerick quickly fails when the story line, rhythm, rhyme or humorous element are not up to scratch. While humour is constructed and arrived at slowly, the rapid flow of words that finally emerge seem paradoxically to be spontaneous and even effortless.

The content of a limerick has a completely different feel to it from a straightforward prose version:

> A player charmed notes from his sensitive parts
> and scored .. every chord with his musical tarts –
> Haydn Brahms Grieg Puccini
> Byrd Purcell and Paganini ...
> the gift .. the drift .. of these magical arts
> grew con brio – orchestrating his farts

The prose version:

An instrumentalist skilfully induced his genitals to play classical compositions by seven composers to the constant delight of his dubious musical female friends. He demonstrated how the seat of his unnatural creative gifts developed in tune with his lively flatulent compositions. (!)

I have written numerous limericks, which have gradually grown increasingly serious and black. Believing that there can be serious limericks I have included a number, especially satirical ones, but it is extremely difficult to decide at what point a limerick turns into a serious poem.

I believe that limericks are all a kind of poetry .. akin to folk art in their vitality, the breadth of their appeal and their earthiness too, emerging prize-less and at best priceless, at the arse end of the real thing.

A quick snack to the novel's six courses, the springing energy of the limerick can crack out like exploding seed-pods. Circling round, fully controlled, it completes itself, carefully closing its own door at exactly the right moment though sometimes with a loud bang. *If a fart should shatter a latitude* is a good example of a first line explosion!

Limericks are loved in their own right. They thrive on an astonishing amount of repetition. Their pounding beat answers the very human need for rhythm, stemming perhaps from the foetus as it experiences the regular beat of its nearby mother's heart.

Experimenting with various verse arrangements gives one an excellent insight into the peculiar nature of the limerick. I have pushed this verse form as far as possible to see just what happens, lengthening, for example, all the lines, or using four short lines instead of two. I have also tried out two long lines to end the verse as you can see in the last example. The possibilities seem endless! You may not end up with a limerick, but with a near relation of real value. And anyway, what does it matter what a verse form is called?

THE LIMERICK'S UNCERTAIN HISTORY

The form of the limerick had been developed by poets long before Lear reinvented it in terms of his childlike whimsical surrealism.

With humour drawn from ever widening sources, the creative and not so creative use of `filth' oozed in, and the standing of the limerick suffered. Well known authors carefully concealed their identity when writing limericks. Prudishness has now lost the influential power it had, and we can be profoundly grateful that the stifling censorship of the recent past is rapidly vanishing.

According to one hotly denied claim, the limerick form was a French invention brought to Ireland in the 17th century by troops commanded by the Earl of Limerick.

Another theory as to who wrote the first recognisable limerick suggests that a sailor who came from that city was the author. Yet another idea as to how they started refers to a pub in Limerick, perhaps at the end of the eighteenth century, where friends tried out their verses on each other. In 1820 the first published limerick told this story of a woman who set out to sea with an owl in a rowing-boat, predating Lear's *The Owl and the Pussycat* by many years:

MISTRESS TOWL

There was an Old Woman named Towl,
Who went out to Sea with her Owl,
    But the Owl was Sea-sick,
    And scream'd for Physic;
Which sadly annoy'd Mistress Towl.

Passing through the city of Limerick recently, I imagined there would be a limerick centre or perhaps a gigantic wall where, along with other visitors, I could spray on my contributions like a graffiti artist. But I just trundled sadly through Limerick without stopping ... quite wordless.

Part
2
EVERMORE
MEANS OUR MURDER
BLINDLY GORGES
THE INNOCENCE
CREATIVE
THE PAGE.

THE LIMERICKS

When his dreamy young dick did the drooop
a camper concockted a loop
but it sank by degrees
squeezed back through his knees
... and drowned without sound in his soup

Strain not! while perfecting the art
of the burp that conceals the fart
a rip-roaring pooper
induces such stupor
deception plays no kind of part!

When a girl freed her soul of all vanity
her friend sneered, "Sheer sexual inanity!
mere whiffs of a sniff on
hypnotic scented chiffon
and the odd sods surrender their sanity "

"POOR PEACOCK! .. dear God! – how absurd!
the nearest to heaven in bird!
... sexual engineering
unbearably wearing ....
.... while your girl pecks about with a turd ... "

A phenomenon typically new –
Dad's too busy to read a book through
one minute so awed
now totally bored ....
....

"Thirty-five thousand facets per eye
not bad for a modest dragonfly!
I've phased my gaze
in a high heady haze
you lovely little lissom ... LAZULI!"

A lady of substance I know
wore a massive lead heart hanging low
... it slipped from her cleavage
ripped right through her sleevage
and vanished from earth with her toe

Birdsong trills up from the bed
of a man fully certified dead
expressing elation
as reincarnation
recycles what used to be Fred

"Excuse me my rude intervention
but beware your lover's intention
might we not find
love not so much blind
as an act of human invention?"

ADDICTED .. to what they thought was new
explorers tried to pothole down the loo ..
this message .. spoiled .. unkind
was toiled back .. soiled .. but signed –
down here it's like a whole damn human zoo

Could LIFE have survived without KILLING?
the guts blood and slaughter ... God willing
my cat has a soul
till he sees a fat vole
... twin pleasures supremely fulfilling!

FILM LOVERS .. have clinched and they've clung!
erotic .. neurotic .... high-strung!
.... good God! – there beneath
the slobber and teeth
he's swallowed her beautiful tongue!

Killer Thumbs Martin .. yes he!
asked, "Who'd like a nice cup of tea?"
Stiletto Joe
politely said "No"
Stocking Garrotte said, "Me"

Obsessed .. and worse .. POSSESSED .. by dammed T.V.
an addict thought in channels .. as you'll see
when his girl .. no 1 or 2
switched on adverts every screw
he checked the ins and outs of 4 and 3

Where all but true craftsmen will fail
is withdrawing snot-flakes with the nail
... superb when intact
perfection in fact
with a trembling green blob in the tail

A young exhibitionist nutter
once leaped from the Eiffel Tower's gutter
his contraption of brollies
fed up with his follies
gained height and flew right to Calcutta!

From sex with no go or firm meaning
our cuntry needs punitive weaning!
systematic sharpish shocks
to disenchanted cocks
should reform their angle of leaning

Dear God! was it some kind of blunder?
that oysters can mate is a wonder
can they be coping
with that gritty .. grotty .. groping?
what's `sideways´ to `over-and-under´?

Crashing again in a stupor
splats that gnat in the same lentil soup .. a
mean farting bean
causing haste quite obscene
in a flying machine
halfway through looping the looper

Fountain cherubs .. peeing free in September
lack the knack of attack by December
... pissing ice snow and hail
to the wail of a gale
cruel fate sets the date ... to dismember!

A tree not especially bright
felt creative one boring black night
so contriving a mystery
and defying plant history
grew eagerly straight for the dark

MAN defines MAN as the-one-who-atones
but we'll all sin-as-one .. as identical clones
collective our luck .. collective our lot
in one last .. vast .. fucking .. melting-pot
same eyes .. same sighs .. same uniform moans

God peers through his tears through the vapours
"My faith in mankind ever tapers
they're all a bit mad
maybe more good than bad
though the good hardly gets in the papers"

THE TABLOIDS TURN SPORT INTO A RELIGION
AND RELIGION INTO A SPORT

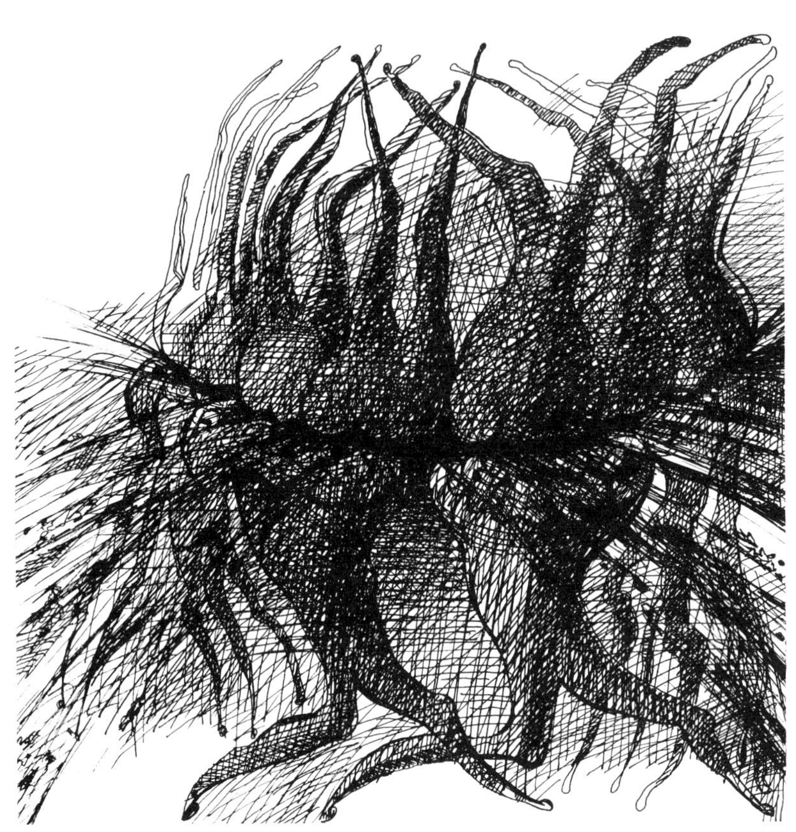

The teeth-wrenching clench on each faceful
took no heed of her need to be graceful
belching and base
was Cruel Gruel Grace
but her guff was a bluff .. and disgraceful!

With that riotous life in a tree
our ancestors couldn't foresee
this life of perdition
IN THE SITTING POSITION
you surely do have to agree

The orgasm .... so so unfair
will it ever .. well .. get anywhere?
first the soft sighing
I'm more or less dying
and it's vanished into thin fucking air

TODAY! .. the deployment of bugs
would transform his quite charming old rugs
yes! .. in spite of the tomes
the good Sherlock Holmes
would be done for – possession of drugs ...

As pigs have a deep feline purr
no farmer with cats could demur
if groaning and red
they heave into bed
their less pussy traits ... so to blur

Whatever she was trying to sell
rushing past I was going like hell
my flailing resistance
subdued her persistence
"Thanks for your time!" came the yell

An elf .. fairy .. an alright sprite
wrote history by pure fairy light
`Insubstantials´ lack invention
MAN you see got not one mention
... a goblin punched one .. he was tight –
he'd seen a routine troll by night

For a national symbol and saint
George showed surprising restraint
the dragon's vast size!
blood-red gorged eyes!
sudden-death cries!
he retreated .. defeated .. to faint

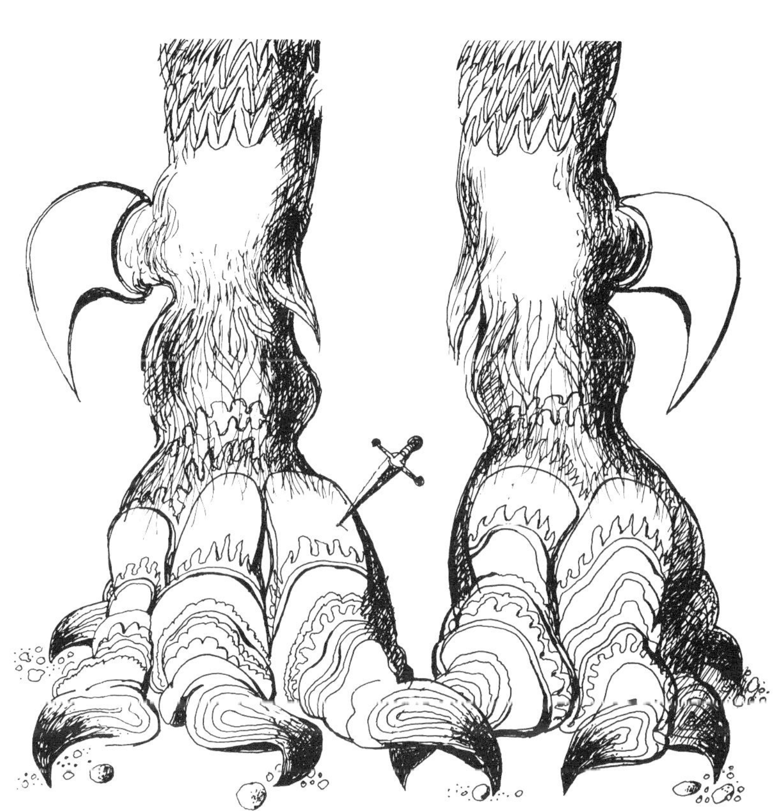

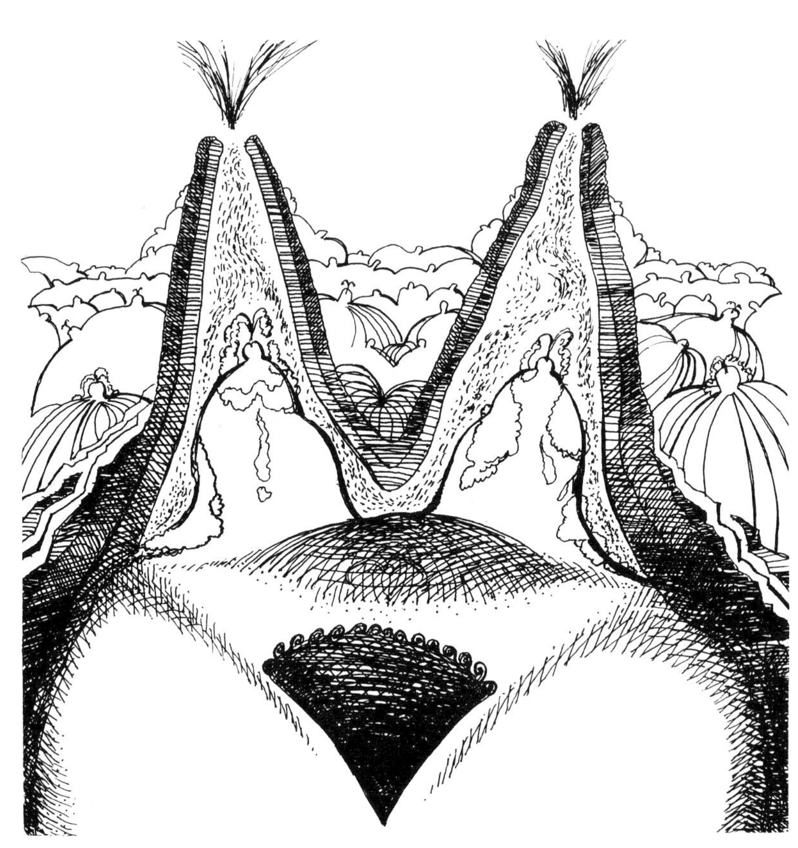

With age-infirm sperm it's a must
contemplating the ripe type of bust
imagined as mountains
with cream-foaming fountains
titillating volcanoes of lust!

Should the praises .. well .. ever be wrung
from fossilised dinosaur dung?
hapless the he who first hit
on priceless immovable shit!
in a word absurd turd .. dung far-flung

Now ladies! ... it leads to perdition
ban Godless unwanted coition
on the point of assaulting
avoid his pole .. vaulting
and mission position submission

"The heavens inspired our thesaurus"
smirked an author, "Prepare to adore us!
once homework was crippling
for parent and stripling
.. the stars solve the entries that floor us –
she's Virgo .. she's Pisces .. I'm Taurus"

A poet could never be curbed
of the hideous way that he verbed!
the nastiest nouning
adjectival clowning
let him create in peace – undisturbed ...

Sighed Zeus, "It seems more than an aeon
the earth's been fit only to pee on!
thank Zeusness up here
I can still breath the air
and the lights on dark nights are not neon"

Working contract fairies with loaded crock of gold
always do ... no striking ... precisely as they're told!
digging at the rainbow's end
grimace to face its aimless trend
... can this really be the goal –
fifty yards of wending hole?
beerless cheerless .. weary fairies .. really CAN grow old

A girl twirled in with the wheeze
of concocting a striptease trapeze!
high hopes snapped drastically
with her knickers elastically
twisting fantastically
and in spite of her three good degrees
her bra fluttered down in Belize

1ST CLASS
DEGREE
PURE MATHS
1ST CLASS
DEGREE
THERMO DYNAMICS
1ST CLASS
DEGREE
KNICKER ELASTIC

The stands at the naval review
groaned with brass-hats in love with the new
but the fabulous ships
had to make thirty trips
now the cuts have reduced them to two

An athlete at a meet in old Samothrace
won first prize .. in disguise .. in a mammoth race
ace too as a Stegosaur
Archaeopteryx .. Minotaur --
a queer hairy pair in a paper-chase!

A seventeenth century teenager
laid a kind of historical wager
"In three hundred years
we'll be diverting our Sirs
in a tit-ring and G-string assuager!"

If Josephine and Marie Antoinette
could compare their massive spending with a bet
well .. Josephine was faster
undisputed master –
a treasury disaster!
so history really owes us quite a debt

"Lose the reins and it's tits over bum
just watching you makes me go numb!
stop jumping – I'll DIE!
and don't you dare cry ...
WIN!!! .. don't be coerced by your Mum!!"

An intelligence averaging nought
achieved what might well have been thought
.. as brain cells grow older
they crumble and moulder –
don't register quite as they ought
to

The mill with its water-worn wheel
met a lifelong .. so longed for .. ideal
the dirt-dusted doors
cracking walls .. gaping floors
sagging beams .. muffled screams –
the authentic historical feel

A cracker seduced by a nut
cries, "Hazel! .. our smut's got a BUT –
a love too external –
no discernible kernel!
... face a case that's both open and shut"

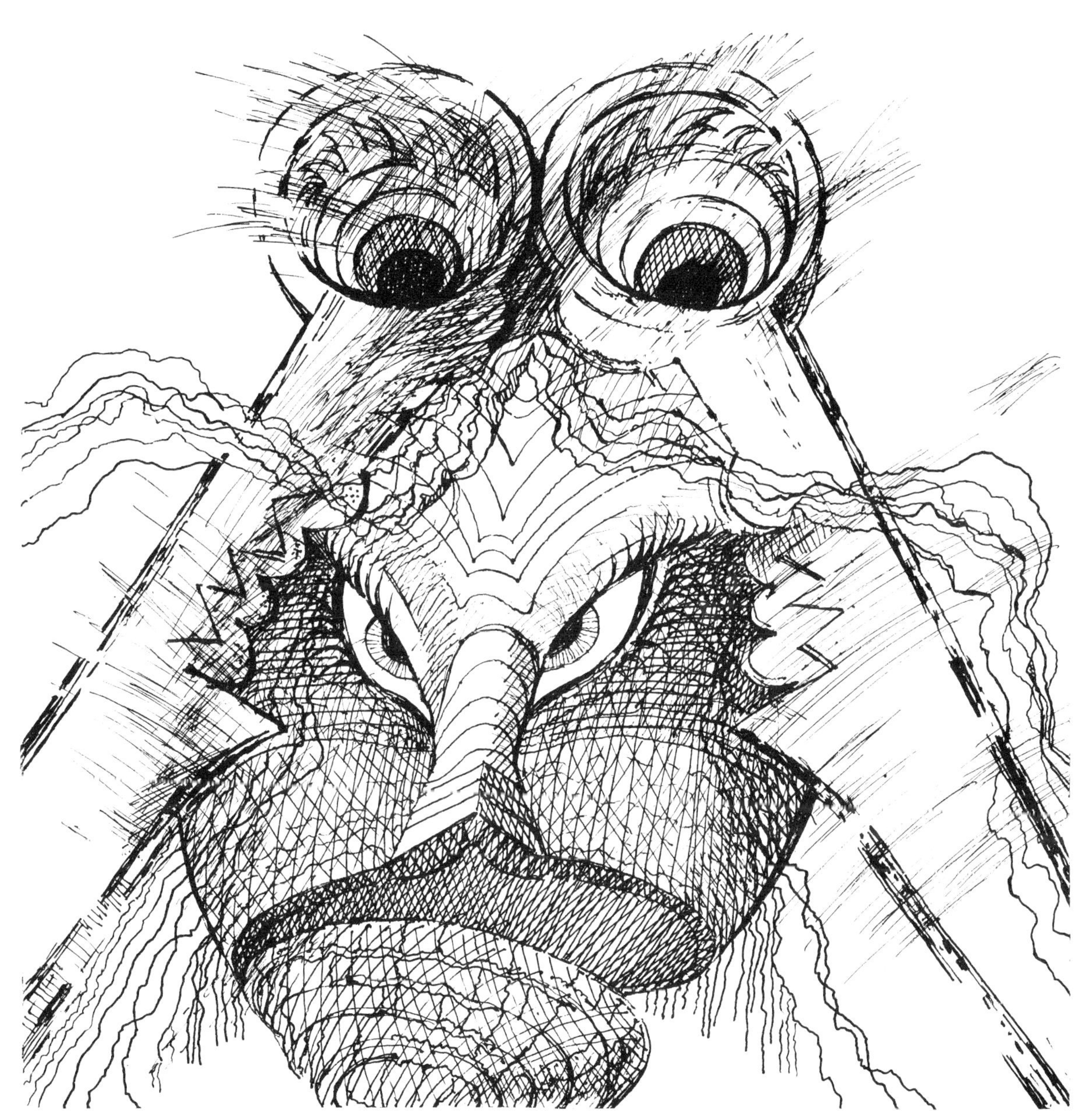

Picking matches up strewn on the floor
an old man creaked, "My favourite chore!
past friends will attest
for CARDIAC ARREST
arching backwards is best
with two match-picking teeth in your jaw"

IRON MUSCLES of progress will flex
to genetically modified sex
... male martyred members
ebbing in the embers –
overbooked .. overcooked – wrecks!

Life's thread in his head in his bed
wasn't lost as he tossed till he said
"I was worried but fine
then that body of mine
with its stink made me think it was dead"

Dried up drinking gallons of wine
in a poet a terminal sign
came a thief in the night
with just the insight
and a perfectly brilliant last line

NELSON .. a-columned .. is head-in-the-sky
from the ground – a tiny `Horatio fly´
necks vent invective
on the killing perspective
... pigeons coo, "WHO gets – one in the eye?"

Her smile is by miles the keenest
her fate to date .. maybe the meanest
in the very JAWSOFDEATH
she gags, "Oh God! – your breath
you're losing a world-class hygienist!"

The enemy aimed to a man
at the rock-like chief of the clan
"Their shooting's a farce!" he sneered
"Out of their arse!" he jeered
"Couldn't hit an elephan -----"

To escape the perpetual rain
some poor sod lived deep down a drain
and grew ever thinner
on six sorts of dinner
... all sodding condoms again

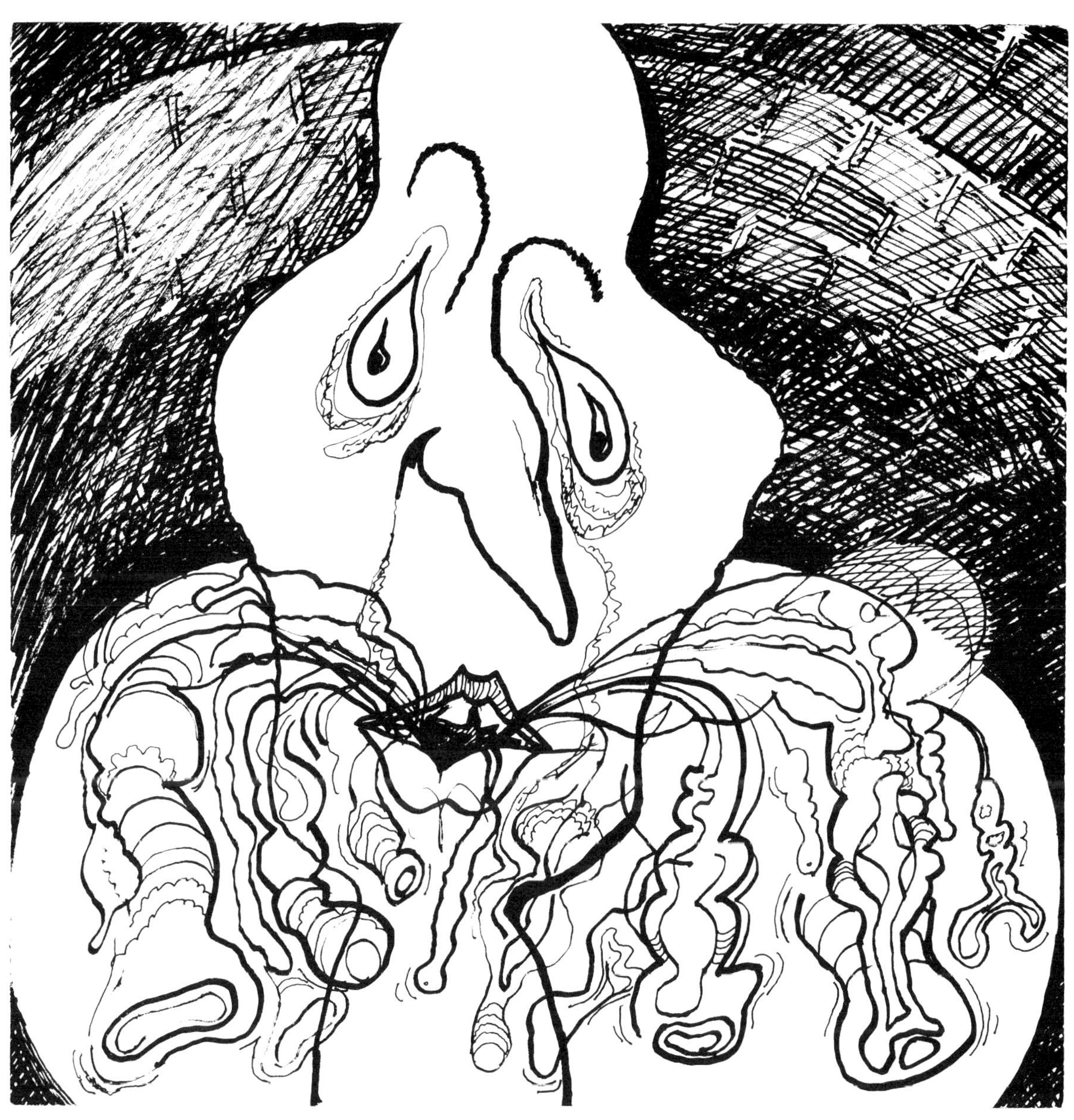

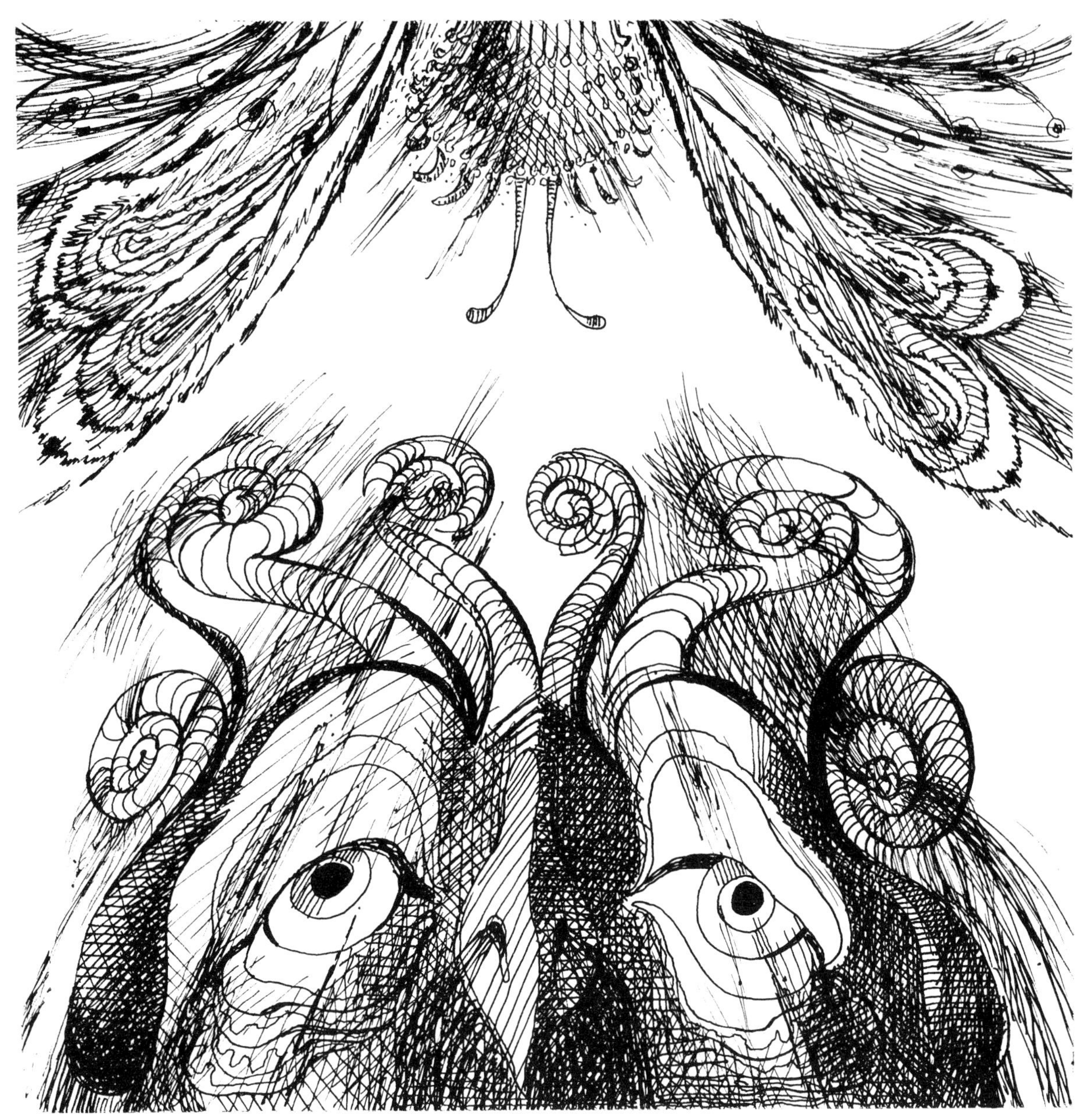

"With this my Olympian eyrie"
warbled Zeus, "I'm parrot-shit weary
my eagle eyes old dim and bleary
... an aerial lurch
I'll fall off my perch
and reincarnate as a fairy"

How humbling to MAN'S worn humanity –
tabloiding into insanity?
deathly a dance
reverse to advance!
and claw our way back to INANITY

Making free with her lover-to-be
with supreme masochistical glee
a girl did the deed
the poor sod on a lead
for the cosmic orgasmic ennui

"Prayers poisoned" sighed God, "By pure hate
have forever flowed fast through my gate
can they not tell
they're sent on to hell?
next Monday – the final send-in date"

"I get burps and bad acid from wine
there's both legs and left kidney of mine
that pounding old pain –
my massive migraine
Oh! – the hormones .... but really I'm fine!"

Locked drivers both blocked in a slot
screeched, "SHITHEAD!!" more often than not
with the road-rage increased
both cars well deceased
there's a near-new second-hand parts lot

It takes a real creative loss adjuster
to puzzle out this missing-half BLOCKBUSTER
you view .... top .... Monet
half
with a free framed hair display
a head-wall .. you could say
with your eyeballs losing all of half their lustre

Bringing death up to date .. The Grim Reaper
is mechanised down to the bleeper
the doom-laden air
is in high-tech despair
robotic .. idiotic .. Grim Weeper

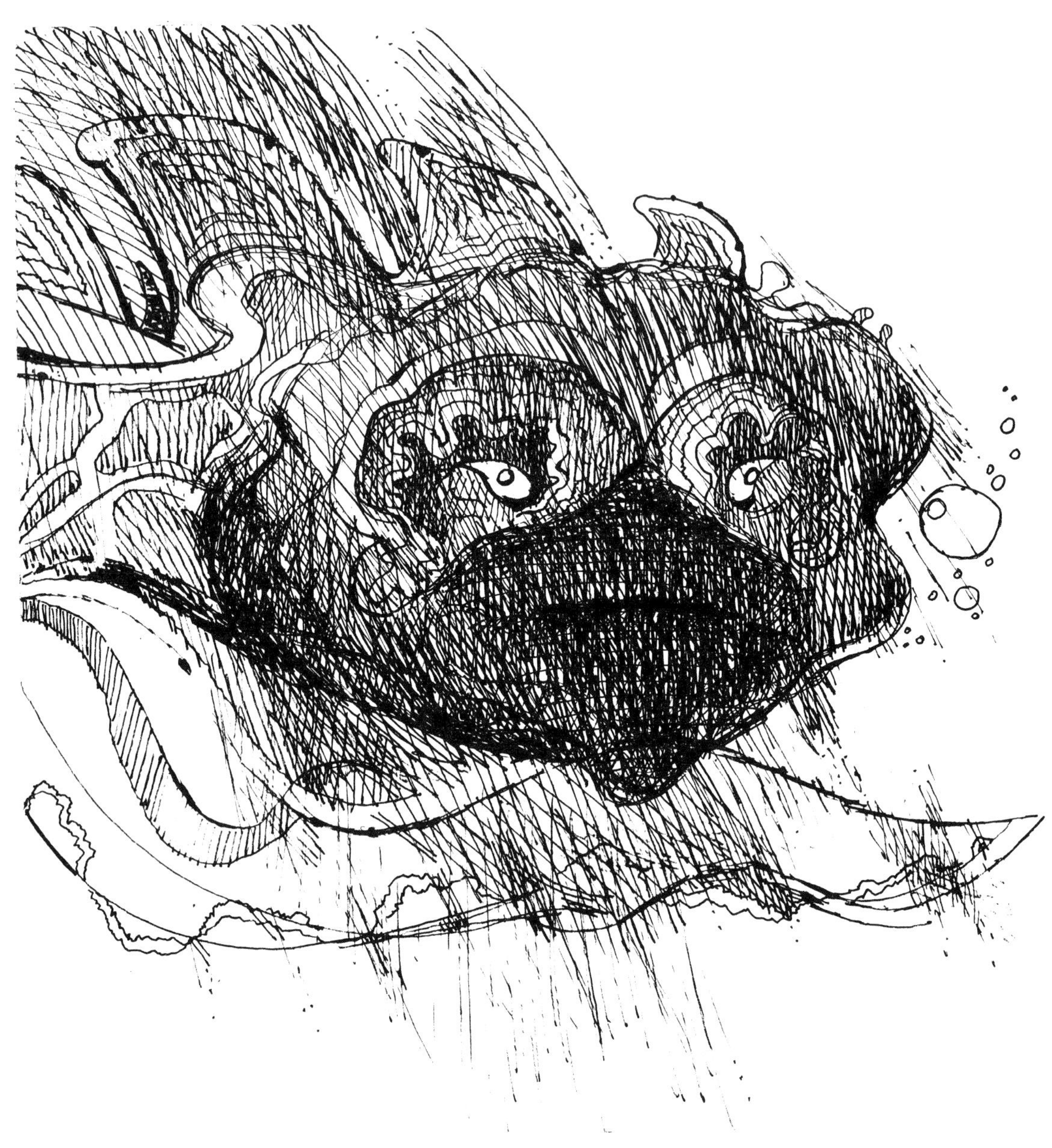

A tadpole far gone in longevity
with horrid and unworthy levity
burbled, "Quick now .. pretty toad
split! splat! splot! across the road
... the beauty of life – blessed brevity"

A writer obsessed with *icx*
wrote – Blast my mind and it's *tricx*
sod! what a *ficx*
when my *dicx* in her *knic*x
if *cunz* and *pricx* don't *micx*

A weirdly extravagant creature
was born with a bi-function feature ...
her nib-of-a-nose
wrote nightmares in prose –
surrealism bedded with Nietsche

The computer clicked, "Eeek .. ick .... Miss Pringle
I'm not selling these tickets as single
the profit .. no trouble
comes selling them double
so mingle Miss Tingle .... Miss Tringle"

A pig-in-a-poke alcoholic
put his best to the test in a frolic
could his girl with a lick
to his dick do the trick
or his prick .. was it purely symbolic?

She sexily gazed in his eyes
"Guys rise to the pump-priming exercise!"
resistance eroded
he swelled up .. exploded
and brought down a small cloud of flies

Battling botty bloodles to the blottlebank ... battlebonk

.... Battling bloody bottles to the bottle-bank
a bemused boozer .. mused .. suffused on whathedrank
he slogged waterlogged and manic
through ranks ti-fucking-tanic
belting, "Bottle all the buggers! ... buck the fottlebank!"

The pianist slumped as though dead
shot by a note through the head
twanged from a harp
in F-fucking sharp
"The finale!" he gasped as he bled

MEOWSE

Extending the latest genetical nous
a doctor re-programmed his spite-spitting spouse
from his non-talking cat
God! who'd think of that?
... he broods on stewed cat food and hot chocolate mouse

VIRGIN GARDEN ... plant this that .. or what?
you plant one of whatever they've got
the resulting confusion
leads to just one conclusion –
you've fucked up a beautiful spot

A guard fell in love with the train
a union we all should disdain
the rolling-tot-stock
clanked out on the clock –
the first machines with a brain

The bog-standard boy from next door
won his girl – an unwavering bore ...
days – dreary .. dull .. depleted
dismal .. dire .. deleted
deadly .. dammed .. defeated –
were all faithfully repeated
... a point they were pleased to ignore!

ALL WRITERS now live in an age
when their words must come up off the page ...
what they call creative
some words find sedative
and sit watching them get in a rage ...

Doctor Spooner glopped, "What - what - what – what'll
stop glottal-stops stopping my glottal?
I'll throw a *felling tit*
and *bash a lout* a bit
... *signed coals* will *unthrottle my bottle*"

Adverts are out in the lead
in creating the virtual need
... the offers .. if various
are often vicarious
for half-witted robots indeed!

My cat sticks his arse in my face
is he playing his only real ace?
does he fear an attack?
should I welcome this kak?
.... am I finally put in my place?

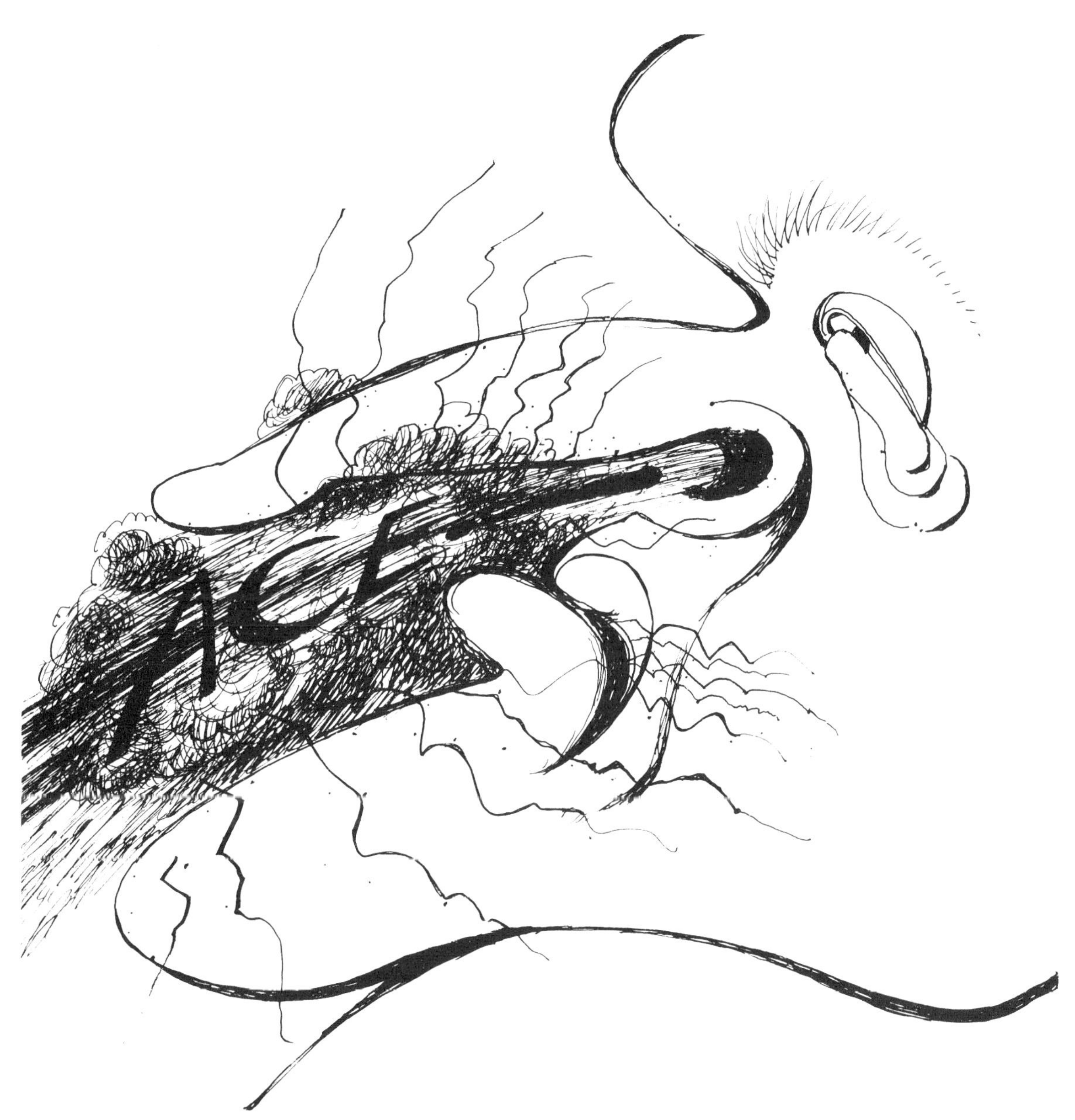

Looking up and forwards .. a priest
said, "One senses some future at least ...
looking downwards and back
with HELL there through a crack
to a-round-the-clock barbeque feast"

A boomerang circling the air
lived for the moment up there
it loved the rotation
the thermal flotation
suppressing the niggling fear –
life's travellers don't get anywhere

A fairy far wiser than some
was born with a centipede's bum
with a witch for a mother
garden gnome for a brother
she takes things just as they come

"You starlings can't personally sing
you do curlew .. hen .. lapwing
imitations man-detected
quite admirably perfected
.... ventrilloquism might be your thing?"

Why in heaven should penguins have knees?
they do not resist heavy seas
but are put there to pray
"In God's name go away!"
("bloody twitchers .. we say
PISS OFF! and just leave us to freeze")

What exactly might farts be expressing?
user friendly .. in fact quite a blessing
amusing .. seductive
some life-force destructive
God knows .. but He's keeping us guessing

A writer sighed, "What can I say?
my work gets .. well .. worse by the day –
lines will keep on rhyming with *Bray!*
my *Brays* being vicarless
what's left but the knickerless –
A sexy young girl from Pompeii ....
gave a red-hot volcanic display...."

They grow so prodigiously pated
untold oldies are follically fated
front and back of the head
could be culled from the dead
from sources .. well .. barely related

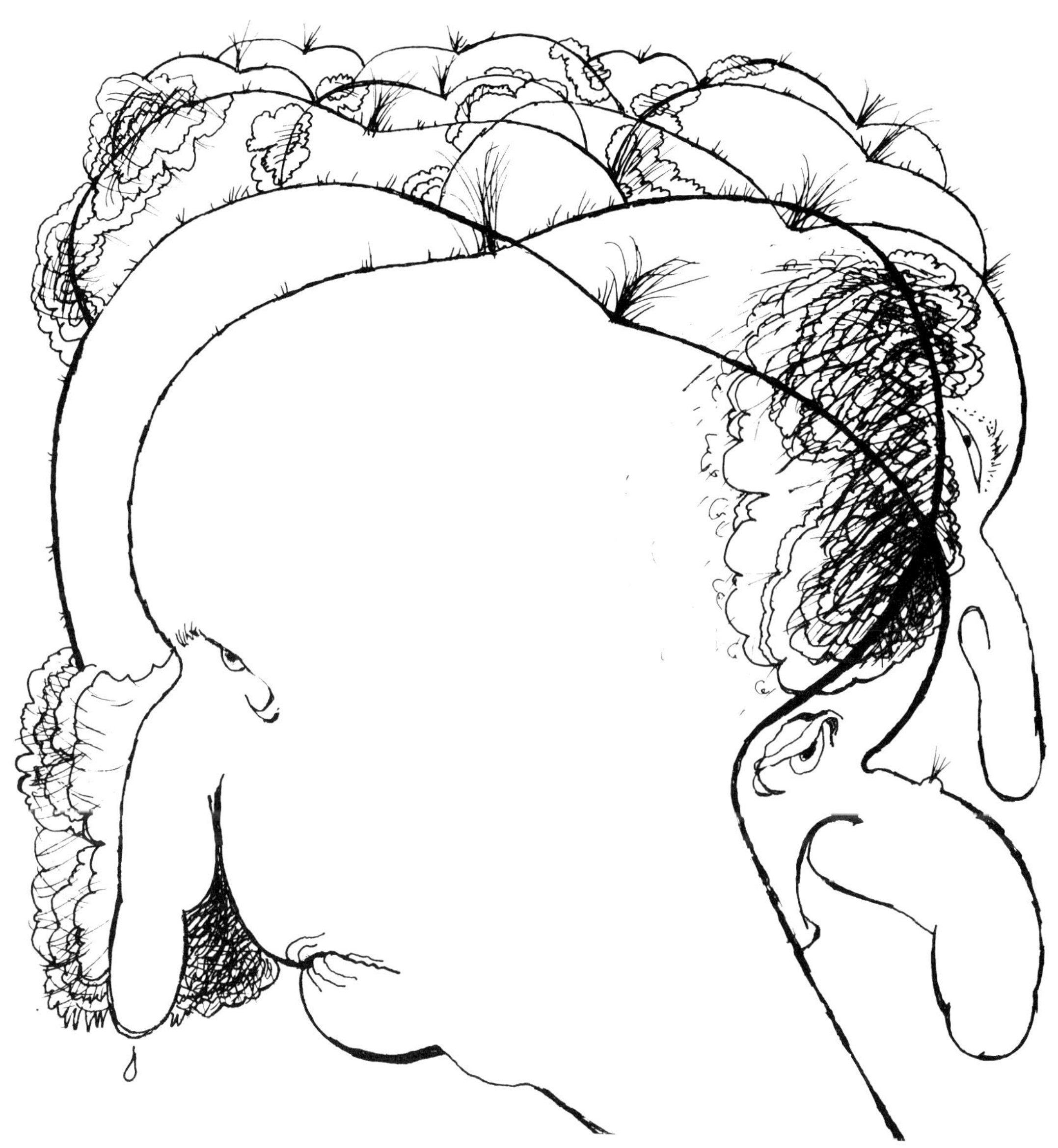

They charge large heaven's gate fees
for the sky-highed sword of Damocles
hanging there ready
and reasonably steady
by – HE! HE! ... who is holding the keys

EVOLUTION ... complex beyond knowing
from dithering single cells flowing
with splitting indecision
for amoebas of vision
knowing not if they're going or coming

"When you're peckish .. there's soggy squashed frog
run-flat rat .. squirrel .. hedgehog
hen .. fox .. sheep .. rabbit
a cheap healthy habit"
he crowed and slogged on with the jog

"For those we are about to deceive
and the tricks still there up our sleeve
make us truly grateful –
this political plateful
we may yet be forced to retrieve!"

Loo skribblers! ... the privvyc's tellin'
yore brane cels carnt coap wiv yor cpellin'
arsewhole krappy finkin'
iz nott aloan stinkin'
wiff luv-berd werd terds ...... soffly wellin'

We lurch in our spiritual search
replacing grimacing in church
with real wallet denters –
dear garden centres
with God in each silvery birch

Starry nights shine their void on the city
man shrinks as he voids on the pity
and he mimics the mole
blcary blind in his hole
locked up in his own nitty-gritty

A man showing off .. I suppose
forced his weird ten tiered beard up his nose
so hard it appears
it squeezed out through his ears
till it tickled the tops of his toes

DO NOT RETURN
TO ZEUS (MT. OLYMPUS)
JUPITER MARS
IF FOUND UNEXPLODED

A sad Ancient Greek cried "How odd!
too true I'm the worst sort of sod
but the thought of it jars –
a bolt came from Mars
that most Roman of stars
... I was killed by the wrong sort of god"

A walker's thighs blocked out the skies ... so vertically elite
he loped and leapt on limbs inept .. the crusty crags of Crete
... engineers were near to tears
a deadline they must meet –
to fathom why he had to fly .... to synchronise his feet

When the great wish they'd only been rash
and are treated to headlines like – TRASH
do please avoid a
smile of schadenfreude
lest your soul find a role as .. say ...... ash?

The Devil de-dribbled and mused
"Technology must now be used
in our most hellish zone
with the mobile phone
for a more modern moan
... they're bored with the way they're abused"

Bugger what's written and said!
today architecture is dead --
fake .. facile and fleeting
fields metalled in sheeting
... vast buildings no more than a shed

News grows more murderously angled
sundry killing .. blood feeding .. the mangled
our tortuous times
blindly gorging on crimes –
our children .. wide-eyed .. web entangled

Words come softly wafting on a slow sane scented swell
and some will reach a heaven .. and some will make a hell
when they screw the word EROTIC
porn-tooled – pornrobotic
to the sweet dead sickly smelling of the lubricating gel

Horned lizards squirt blood from their eyes!
should girls repel sex in this guise
and learning the knack
to counter-attack
when they're fed all the usual lies?

A back-racking black widow spider
sucked failed .. impaled males .. deep inside 'er
this prick-prodding passion
fairly fucked .. in the fashion
each mate .. who felt great .. till 'e eyed 'er

A LABORATORY .. flushed down the loo
kills germs .... but what about you?
with ads thick and fast
are you sure you can last?
.... your IMMUNITY .. may have a view!

Slipping home from a blinder .. a bender
crept a boozer remorsefully tender ..
his wife shouted, "LUKE!
if it's you in the PUKE –
I'll be your hidden agenda!"

The universe cools .. with our trust
and we're stuck on this small speck of dust ..
galactical leanings
from optical gleanings
lack visible meanings
...... dare .. DARE we hope God's got it sussed?

"Checking your equipment .. calculate the rule
for a life spent pissing in an average pool
correctly assess
would it fill it .. more or less?
top marks require a really first class tool"

"I can see right through you .. I find"
beamed the psychic ... "God's gift I'm assigned"
his client .. if blighted
was simply delighted
and her family .. sitting behind

In the absence of moral compunction
at this mystic millennium junction
we are doubled in doubt
at to WHAT we're about
disengaged from the Deity's function

"EXPENSES!" moaned Santa, "Are chronic!
gifts – insane .. dear .. electronic
... imagine the night –
a tax on each flight
and toy jets whizzing past – SUPERSONIC!"

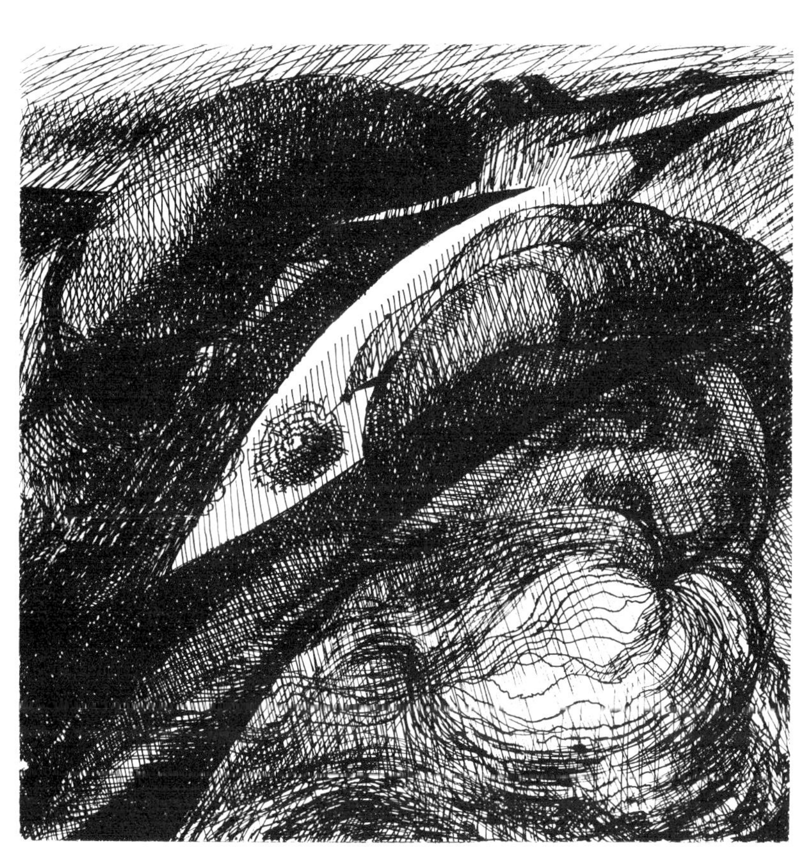

LOOK WHAT I VE FOUND, EVE

"I'm dreading this shedding and shedding my sin"
hissed the snake, "along with the discarded skin
... a moral compulsion
since the shocking EXPULSION
that snake only shouted, `Hey! coxes are in´"

A man won first prize in his section
for his fine architectural erection!
girls from all lands
stood silent in the stands
quite lost in dense clouds of reflection ...

If a fart should shatter a latitude
the attitude could be a platitude –
sheer dedicated sneeriness
bored flawed world weariness
reacting with grating ingratitude!

It's so easy to empty the seas
Man can do it with consummate ease
nearly all of the cod
is killed off .. and God
will become even harder to please

A writer politically correct
spoke swear words too soft to detect
as he started to shout
"FROG! WOG! CUNT! KRAUT!"
... in a voice of the utmost respect ...

Where's the sense then in – taking a pee
is our language right out of its tree?
the essence is this –
when we're all full of piss
expect a catastrophe!

Hunting down all those innocent mice
is not nice in a PUSS PARADISE
feed each need – post-material
with thoughts more ethereal
and remember ... cats only live twice

LIFE CREATED – flesh and love .. amino acids .. fats
spread abroad perfection .... except bubonic rats ..
sharks .. pike .. fleas .. piranhas
midges .. scorpions .. old bananas
A PARADISE FOR LICE ... VICE ... SATANIC VAMPIRE BATS

In underwear not strictly there .. she'd snare her Mister Right
the New Year throng .. all Mister Wrong .. were really wrong that night
they lewdly leered .. they crudely cheered
outsize eyes she flashed and flared!
weird sheared TEETH she bleakly bared!
... and knobs .. with sobs and baggy bits ... began to disunite ...

Muddled .. huddled .. fuddled .. in God's own waiting womb
(damn! damn! damn! try again, er) .. God's own waiting room
trying to see the light
it's – WHAM! .. eternal night!
...... an awesome spirit figure beckons through the gloom
vaguely `Father Christmas´ .. with added sonic boom ...

The doctor called, "Here's the analysis!
you've caught – `phaeochromocytomalysis´"
... the patient had heard
but breathing no word
died of – pathological-terminology-paralysis!

"Ring this man of spirit and vision
ignoring the misplaced derision!"
.. the voice on the phone –
"I'm here on my own
my soul's out on loan
and my body won't make a decision"

Did he dream of esteem as he sawed?
are they paid-for these snores of a lord?
... bringing faceless disgrace
on that far off `other place´
... the terminal land of the bored?

An angel thought – God! it's a farce!
trapped here a sculpture in brass
a spiritual ministry
lasts for infinitry
... but only the perfect can pass

COMMOM ANGEL ENTRANCE EXAMINATION

1. "You are a *perfect* angel!"
   How many times in your life has your behaviour provoked this enchanting endearment?

2. Name at least fifty-two stages in elementary halo maintenance.

3. Mach 1, mach 2, mach 3, mach 4.
   At which of these airspeeds can a feckless angel expect a bout of winglessness?

4. Plummeting out of control, the wind screaming through your golden hair, would you make any retrieved wing fragments serviceable with:
   a. balsa wood   b. sheet metal   c. prayer   d. clingfilm?

5. All angels in paintings look disconcertingly similar. You can only tell an angel's gender by observing whether he/she is using a spear and sword dealing out death, or God – to heal someone.

   To simplify this problem should :
   a. male angels grow beards
   b. all angels be unisex?
   c. unconditional disarmament be enforced?

6. As angels are clearly all under twenty-five, does this incline you to favour positive discrimination for the elderly?

7. If your answer to the last question is "Yes", would you still hold this view if you were a million year old angel dragging on and on forever, constantly forgetting whether you were catholic or protestant, incapable of sustained flight or getting – "Hallelulia" ... er ... "Hallelujah" right?

(Enquiries and litigation in respect of these questions should be addressed to your Ombodsgod.)

Signed : Mark   *Mark*   (P.P. Administering Angel)

To my cat – a whole barrage of lies
wouldn't come as the slightest surprise!
it might sound inept
but to simply accept
is the reason he always looks wise

Willing girls are not gilding the lily
flaunting lingerie dauntingly frilly
hauls of mauled balls
installed in their smalls
make them wear their queer gear .. willy-nilly

Man's sense of his inner reality
and feeling for self-immortality
are interrelated
spiritually weighted
ensuring enduring fatality

This film ... God! .. what it entails –
ripped-apart dubious males!
are the guts of a hood
so finger lickin' good
LIFE – no more than the gore and the sales?

DRAWN HEROES .. hate cartoon castration!
and it's hopeless for sex education
their off-spring production
a shocking misconstruction
is a cop-out for pop copulation

Film thugs are mugs .. there is no future in it
this cop war bore
directors always win it –
when they're aiming at a STAR
crooks can hardly hit the car
though they're blasting off with tons of lead a minute!

Perverse .. in reverse .. it baldly needs re-stating
LIFE'S only happy when deteriorating ...
uncouth youth!
face the awful truth
your barely bloody born .. and the next world's waiting

Slow ageing .. to the aged .. is hideous
not exempting the ultra fastidious!
fading flaccid faces see
mirrored back .. an unknown `me´
NATURE .. so sweet .. and invidious

In the breathless silent vistas of the dead
my heaven-sent bright symbol of a bed
looks down upon an ocean
of frenetic self-promotion
from which .. dear God .. I hope my spirit's fled!